is nothing in this world with more currency than kindness. But how do we balance being compassionate without letting people take advantage of us? Just as an aggressive, shouty leader does not bring out the best in people, a compassionate leader must still hold individuals to account, make tough decisions, and be willing to be disliked. This balance can be challenging and certainly has been for me at times. How can we balance the values of kindness while ensuring we do what's best for the organisation? This book will explore what it means to be a compassionate leader and how you can achieve this without being seen as a pushover or ineffective.

Throughout my career, the managers who had the most impact on me were those who were kind – they took the time to get to know me, listened, gave me trust and provided opportunities for me to develop. Being treated with kindness is a huge motivating factor for me, encouraging me to work hard, take risks and "go the extra mile" for the organisation. I have come to appreciate the impact of kindness in the workplace and now see it as a superpower. As I have trusted myself to be myself, I have observed a shift in culture within my workplace. Kindness is contagious, others see the power of kindness in engaging with people and lead with this too.

Leading With Heart

Introduction: What is Compassionate Leadership?

For a long time in my first management role, I felt like a fraud. I believed that effective managers were loud, confident to stand in a crowded room to defend their point and made tough decisions without hesitation. I was a long way from brash and bold, but brash and bold was what I thought my organisation wanted– both the board that employed me and the staff team I led. This belief persisted even though these were not the behaviours of the leaders who had the biggest positive impact in my life. In fact, the qualities they exhibited were the opposite of those described above. I grew up in the 1980s, a time when managers portrayed in the media, on TV and in films were overwhelmingly male, abrasive, hostile, uncaring, and focussed on results and not people. Female leaders were in a minority and those that did exist were encouraged to behave like their male counterparts. I understand now how this shaped by perception of a "good" and "worthy" manager. My leadership style was so far from this perception, resulting in me spending a long time feeling inadequate whilst trying (and failing) to act the part of the image of a "good" manager in my head.

As a new manager I would sit in meetings with leaders from other organisations and wish I could be more forthright and militant. It took me longer than it should have, but over time, I came to recognise that the leaders who made the most noise, didn't always make points of value. Those individuals who confidently jumped in with a counter argument against a proposal often hadn't listened to what was being said or failed to recognise the bigger picture. Meanwhile, the work I had been quietly doing to improve my team's efficiency, enhance the culture, and implement clearly defined policies and procedures was beginning to pay off. Stakeholders started to notice the positive and welcoming environment I had created. They saw that our organisation could be relied upon to complete high-quality work efficiently. I realised that I didn't need a loud voice; I just needed to share my passion, be consistent and operate with integrity. People could see for themselves what was being achieved, and I was building the organisation's reputation.

At best, a leader is charismatic, inspiring, responsive, intelligent, and both trusted and trusting. Such a leader influences and supports others to work towards a shared goal. The results are high productivity, high staff morale, low staff turnover, and improved quality. An ineffective or incapable leader has the opposite impact on the organisation. In such situations, staff motivation is low, absenteeism and turnover are high, productivity is low, costs are high, and goals are not being achieved. So, what are the behaviours and skills evident in effective leaders? How does a leader's individual style impact those working in the organisation?

In this book I will share the qualities and approaches I have learned to embrace during my leadership journey over the last twenty years. By putting people at the core of our decision making, we create a culture where employees are motivated to do their best. The techniques I have used to strike a balance between organisation and individual, kindness and accountability will assist new and experienced leaders in creating an environment where they are respected, effective but not feared.

What is a Compassionate Leader?

The compassionate leader brings softer, more traditionally feminine qualities to the workplace and focuses on having a motivated team rather than an intimidated one. Such leaders think about those around them, behave in ways that make others feel valued, cared for, and motivated. A compassionate leader is interested in their employees and the people important to their employees. They seek to support others to achieve their personal and professional goals. It took me years to see kindness as a superpower rather than a weakness. As I have got older and gained life and work experience, I have come to realise that there

CHAPTER 1: THE POWER OF EMPATHY IN LEADERSHIP

Throughout my career, I have been fortunate to work under some truly remarkable managers who still influence my daily decisions as a leader, many years later. While I may not recall every detail of those experiences, what stands out is how these leaders made me feel: respected, listened to, valued, and invested in. This in turn motivated me to excel, live up to the trust they had placed in me, and contribute positively to the team.

What set these inspirational leaders apart? Beyond their competence in our field— in my view a non-negotiable for any leader—they were profoundly human. What I mean by this is they were vulnerable, relatable, supportive, and inspirational.

Empathy: The Heartbeat of Effective Leadership

Empathy, at its core, is the ability to understand and share another's feelings. As leaders, empathy allows us to see the world through the eyes of our team members, creating deep connections and build trust. When employees feel understood and valued, they are more engaged, motivated, and loyal to the organisation. It is possible to wield authority without raising your voice, ruling through fear, or micromanaging.

The link between empathetic leadership and positive organisational outcomes is well-documented. For instance, Sanja Zivkovic, in the 2022 *article Empathy in Leadership: How it Enhances Effectiveness* (available at Empathy in Leadership: How it Enhances Effectiveness (researchgate.net) revealed that employees with empathetic leaders reported lower levels of stress and burnout, alongside higher psychological well-being, and job satisfaction. These leaders were adept at recognising and addressing both the personal and professional needs of their employees, cultivating a healthier work environment. In practice this means leaders at every level taking the time to build relationships with their team, taking the time to ask questions about their lives and sharing details of the leader's own life. Thus, empathetic leadership contributes to better employee well-being, a healthier organisational culture, and tangible business improvements. Those Monday morning conversations about what everyone did at the weekend can on the surface appear to be a frivolous waste of time, but I believe they are crucial in enabling colleagues to understand and have empathy for one another. Those ten minutes taken to say hello and check in with people in the morning is a worthwhile investment, which connects employees to you as an individual as well as the organisation you represent.

Empathy is also crucial for conflict resolution. It fosters mutual respect and encourages open communication. When members of a team feel connected to one another, understand each other's roles and the interplay between them, they are more likely to seek to understand behaviour, rather than jump to a negative viewpoint.

As leaders, it is vital to understand the impact of our decisions on employees' lives and to support them through these changes. While not all decisions can be made solely for employees' benefit—leaders must balance the needs of various stakeholders such as business owners, customers, and funders—it is our responsibility to consider the impact on our teams and mitigate, as far as possible, any negative effects. This is more easily achieved when you know your team and the people, values and goals that are important to them. For example, an organisational restructure requiring redundancies can feel vastly different for an employee who feels consulted, heard, and understood. This means genuinely listening during consultations, providing clear explanations for decisions, and offering support for those affected, such as help in finding new employment. When we understand why a decision has been made, even when it is not the outcome we wanted, it can help to accept the reality of the situation and respect the decision maker. Resentment is bred when individuals do not trust the process and motivation of decision makers.

Cultivating Empathy in Leadership

Empathy can be developed through intentional practice and reflection. The following strategies will help you become a more empathetic leader:

Active Listening: Focus attentively on what others are saying without interrupting or judging. Paraphrase and reflect on their thoughts and emotions to show understanding and validation.

Perspective-taking: Put yourself in your team members' shoes to understand their experiences and viewpoints. Consider their backgrounds, motivations, and challenges to appreciate their unique circumstances.

Emotional Intelligence: Become attuned to your own emotions and those of others. Recognise and regulate your emotional responses to foster deeper connections. This may mean not responding to a question or comment immediately, but stating to the employee you will come back to them once you have considered a response.

Empathy-building Activities: Incorporate activities into team meetings and training sessions to promote understanding and collaboration. Encourage sharing personal stories and practicing active listening.

The Insights Discovery Model

I have found the Insights Discovery Model helpful in understanding and appreciating different personalities in the workplace. The model is a personality assessment tool based on Carl Jung's Psychology and has been developed by *Insights Learning & Development Ltd (www.insights.com)*. The Insights Model helps individuals and organisations improve communication, teamwork, and self-awareness through a colour-coded system representing different personality types and preferences. In summary, the model has the following key components to describe how individuals behave in the workplace:

- **Fiery Red**: Assertive, determined, direct, and action oriented.
- **Sunshine Yellow**: Sociable, dynamic, enthusiastic, and persuasive.
- **Earth Green**: Supportive, patient, caring, and harmony-seeking.
- **Cool Blue**: Analytical, precise, cautious, and detail focused.

The model places individuals on a personality wheel that combines these energies, visualising how different personality types can complement or clash with each other. Participants receive a Personal Insights Profile, providing feedback on their strengths, weaknesses, communication styles, and areas for development. This promotes greater self-awareness and personal growth.

Application in the Workplace:

- **Team Development**: Understanding diverse strengths and working styles fosters better collaboration and productivity.
- **Leadership Effectiveness**: Leaders can adapt their styles to motivate and engage their teams more effectively.

- **Improved Communication**: Recognising and adapting to different communication styles leads to more harmonious interactions.
- **Conflict Resolution**: Understanding underlying personality differences helps resolve tensions.

Leaders strong in red or blue are naturally process-focused, while those strong in green and yellow prioritise people. Red or blue-focused leaders risk neglecting the human impact of decisions, potentially demotivating employees. Conversely, green, and yellow-focused leaders might overemphasise individual impact at the expense of broader organisational needs. A balanced approach is best, starting with recognising your natural leadership style and biases. Learning about the insights model and where I sit in it (green!) helped me to appreciate my strengths in supporting people and understand why I have had to work so hard on holding others to account. It gave me the tools to think about my leadership style in a less emotive and negative way. Rather than telling myself I was not very good at challenging others, I learnt to appreciate that this is something I do not enjoy because I prefer a calm, conflict free environment. I can also appreciate that I need to become "redder" to deal with a difficult situation and consider what qualities and behaviours I need to bring to the fore and consciously adopt to manage the situation. Within my organisation gaining an understanding of the model has helped colleagues appreciate others working styles, identifying how individuals with different working styles can work well together. The model provides a common language and shared understanding – we are all different, and bring a diverse range of approaches, skills, and qualities to the team, resulting in us being stronger together.

Conclusion

Embracing empathy is crucial for building strong relationships which drive organisational success and create a culture of trust and collaboration. By connecting with team members on a personal level, leaders can cultivate environments where individuals feel valued, supported, and empowered to achieve their full potential. Through ongoing commitment and practice, empathy can become not just a guiding principle but a transformative force that enriches the lives of both leaders and their teams.

Practical Actions:

- **Spend some time reflecting (or journalling) on the leaders who have had the greatest impact on you.** What qualities did these leaders share? What is your leadership style? What qualities or skills do you want to explore or develop?

- **Explore the Insights Model**: Use this tool to better understand your team and adjust your leadership style. Go to www.insights.com

- **Show Your Humanness**: Let team members see your human side by sharing something of your life outside work and acknowledging mistakes and struggles, fostering trust and relatability.

CHAPTER 2: SETTING CLEAR BOUNDARIES

In the dynamic landscape of leadership, setting clear boundaries is not about building walls; it is about creating frameworks that foster respect, productivity, and mutual understanding. In this chapter, I will explore the significance of boundary-setting in compassionate leadership and provide actionable strategies to effectively communicate expectations while maintaining empathy.

Learning the Hard Way

As a new manager, I was guilty of not enforcing boundaries and letting some employees get away with poor performance and behaviour. I chose to turn a blind eye to their lack of effort to avoid confrontation and, if I'm honest, to be liked. However, this only created resentment within the team and eroded their confidence in me. The poor performance I ignored was visible to everyone else.

What I also came to learn was that poor attitude and performance can be contagious—seeing colleagues get away with doing a bad job is hardly motivational! It took another manager joining the team who was a process driven red, a stark contrast to my gentle people focussed green, to teach me that holding people to account, though uncomfortable in the short term, is far better for everyone in the long term. I realised I had to face issues head-on; leaving them to fester only made them messier and more complex. Whilst dealing with capability or disciplinary issues should, by definition, never be a welcome experience, like most skills, it becomes easier with practice.

Understanding the Importance of Boundaries

Boundaries define acceptable behaviour, roles, and responsibilities within a team or organisation. They provide clarity and structure, empowering individuals to navigate their professional interactions with confidence and integrity. Where boundaries or expectations are explicit, they become part of the shared language and culture of the team, making it easier for colleagues to challenge each other when they observe poor practice or behaviour. In the context of compassionate leadership, establishing boundaries is essential for creating a supportive environment where team members feel valued, heard, and respected. One way to achieve this is by having a set of behavioural and functional standards in the Employees Handbook and displayed on the wall. By doing this leaders are openly stating how they expect employees to work in full view of colleagues and clients, inviting them to challenge if individuals fall short of this commitment.

Promoting Respect and Productivity

Clear boundaries promote respect by defining the parameters of acceptable conduct and interactions. When expectations are clearly communicated and understood, team members are less likely to overstep boundaries or engage in behaviours that may compromise trust or collaboration. Moreover, boundaries create a framework for accountability, ensuring that all team members are held to consistent standards of behaviour and performance. Having policies and procedures in place ensures that issues are responded to consistently and employees know what to expect from managers.

Consider my friend's experience with a manager who said yes to every request she made:

"Can I work from home every Thursday?"

"Yes."

"Can I leave at 2:30 PM every day to collect my children from school?"

"Yes."

"Can I stop doing my weekly administrative tasks and pass them onto my colleague?"

Yes"

Whilst my friend felt they had won the boss lottery, the situation caused enormous resentment within the team. The work in question was in a mental health service where workload couldn't be easily predicted so whilst working from home and leaving early worked well for her, it placed her colleagues under additional pressure. Her colleagues felt undervalued because they were left to pick up the slack. Flexibility can be great, and I do believe that organisations should be as flexible as possible and endeavour to meet employees' requests. However, employers should be consistent in their approach and consider how requests will impact on other members of the team. The truth is that not all roles are compatible with working from home, but in this instance, there may have been a scenario where it worked well if other members of the team were consulted and everyone given the opportunity to benefit from this flexible approach, so that perks and pressures were shared. My belief is that this manager enjoyed being liked and didn't want to jeopardise their positive relationship with my friend by not agreeing to her requests, but they did not consider the implications for the wider team.

Communicating Expectations with Empathy

Effective boundary-setting requires leaders to communicate expectations firmly but with empathy. While it is essential to uphold standards of conduct and performance, it's equally important to recognise the individual needs and circumstances of team members. Approaching boundary-setting with empathy demonstrates an understanding of the challenges and pressures individuals may face, fostering a culture of support and compassion.

For instance, if an employee had recently experienced a bereavement, a compassionate leader would expect this to impact their performance and give them space to address it before raising the issue gently in a one-to-one meeting. Leaders should seek to understand what is going on for the individuals in their team and any drop in standard or performance be met with enquiry and concern in the first instance. That having been said, issues relating to performance or behaviour should not be left unaddressed, as previously noted, others will be watching, however they should be addressed with care.

Providing context and rationale behind rules or guidelines is a key aspect of communicating boundaries empathetically. When team members understand the reasoning behind certain boundaries or policies, they are more likely to comply willingly and feel a sense of ownership in upholding them. Additionally, leaders should be open to feedback and willing to adjust boundaries in response to evolving needs or circumstances, demonstrating flexibility and adaptability.

Ensuring Understanding of Kindness and Resolve

In setting clear boundaries, it is essential for leaders to strike a balance between kindness and resolve. While compassion and empathy are the foundations of compassionate leadership, they must be complemented by a firm commitment to upholding standards and expectations. Leadership can feel remarkably like parenting—children may react strongly against boundaries but enforcing them makes them feel safe and secure. Similarly, while difficult conversations may be uncomfortable, the workplace is a better environment when standards are explicit and consistently applied.

One effective strategy for ensuring that team members understand both kindness and resolve is to lead by example. When leaders consistently model respectful behaviour and adhere to established boundaries, they set a positive precedent for their team to follow. This will be the focus of another chapter in this book.

Conclusion

Setting clear boundaries promotes respect, productivity, and mutual understanding. By establishing frameworks that delineate acceptable behaviour and expectations, leaders create a supportive environment where team members can thrive and achieve their full potential. Through effective communication, empathy, and a balanced approach to kindness and resolve, leaders can cultivate a culture of accountability, respect, and collaboration that drives organisational success.

Practical Actions:

- **Don't put off difficult conversations** - I have found that writing a script for myself in advance can be helpful in these situations. If difficult conversations make you feel uncomfortable, it can be natural to soften your language, and the meaning of your words gets diluted and lost. Having a script which encompasses what I need to say keeps me on track and I find saying the words aloud in preparation, makes them easier to say in the meeting.
- **Model the Behaviour You Want to See**: Always be respectful, treat others with kindness, look for the positives, and do what you say you will.
- **Ensure Clear Policies and Procedures**: Establish and follow clear guidelines to ensure everyone knows where they stand. Be explicit about the standards of behaviour and performance that you expect from the team.

CHAPTER 3: CULTIVATING TRUST

Trust is the cornerstone of effective leadership, serving as the foundation upon which strong relationships and high-performing teams are built. In this chapter, we explore the essential principles for fostering trust within your team. By embodying honesty, reliability, transparency, and integrity, you can earn the trust and respect of your colleagues, laying the groundwork for success.

The Significance of Trust

Trust is the currency of leadership, vital for creating an environment where individuals feel safe, valued, and empowered to contribute their best efforts. When trust is present, team members are more likely to collaborate openly, communicate honestly, and take calculated risks. Conversely, a lack of trust can erode morale, breed uncertainty, and impede progress.

Creating a human-centric environment means accepting that mistakes will be made. In an environment of trust, we want employees to feel able to acknowledge their mistakes and bring them to their leaders' attention. This approach limits the impact of the mistake for both the individual and the organisation and fosters a culture of learning and growth.

Reflecting on personal experience, I've seen how punitive attitudes toward mistakes can be detrimental. Following a disciplinary process, despite an employee's genuine acknowledgment of their error and steps to correct it, can lead to a loss of motivation and trust. Just because we can implement a disciplinary process, doesn't mean we should. However, this needs to be balanced with the seriousness of the issue, the context of situation and the employee's length of service and conduct to date.

The insights model from Chapter 1 can help us understand different approaches to responding to mistakes made by employees. A leader with a red dominant style may follow the process, often overlooking the individual's context and their relationship with the organisation. Conversely, a green dominant leader focuses on the individual and their relationship, potentially avoiding necessary disciplinary actions to maintain harmony. As is often the case, a balanced approach, considering all perspectives before making an informed decision, is usually best.

The key question for me is, what would we gain by putting the individual through a disciplinary process, particularly if they have already learnt from and acknowledged their error? There will of course be situations where the breach of trust is so serious or the impact on others so significant that the incident needs marking. There are also situations where a matter shows a wilful disrespect for the organisation and its people. On such occasions leaders should not shy away from acting. I would encourage leaders when faced with a potential disciplinary to take time and HR advice to consider whether the matter can be dealt with another way. I have been swept up in the moment of dealing with someone's mistake and have gone down the path of disciplinary because it's felt like the "thing I should do," even though at no point did it feel like "the right thing to do." So, trust your instinct and what you know about the individual concerned. If you lean towards a green personality, ask yourself the question "am I giving myself an out because this feels like a hard task?" If it feels right to go ahead do so, knowing that you have fully considered your options. Chances are the member of staff will also understand why the decision was made to instigate disciplinary procedures.

The Role of Communication in Building Trust

Communication is crucial to creating trust. Without it, unhelpful assumptions about others' motivations can lead to suspicion and mistrust. Leaders might fall into the trap of assuming their actions are self-explanatory, believing others will automatically see their efforts as aligned with organisational goals. The truth is, if you don't communicate your intentions, people will draw their own, often incorrect, conclusions.

Leaders' behaviour is always under scrutiny. It is essential to act with integrity if you want to build trust. Credibility is established by doing what you say you will and treating others with fairness and respect. When trust erodes, it's usually due to a series of small incidents rather than dramatic events. I once had a manager who never followed through on actions from our one-to-one meetings. These were not serious issues, but over time, his failure to follow through on small promises, like forwarding an email or bringing in a book, made me feel unimportant and unvalued. This eroded my motivation and made me question his sincerity and commitment.

As a leader, you are a role model. Your behaviour sets the tone for the organisational culture and demonstrates how to embody the organisation's core values.

Embodying Honesty, Reliability, and Transparency

At the heart of trust-building lies a commitment to honesty, reliability, and transparency. Leaders who communicate openly and candidly with their team foster an environment of trust and accountability. By sharing relevant information, providing timely feedback, and addressing concerns openly, leaders demonstrate respect for their team members and cultivate a culture of transparency. A few years ago, we had a serious incident at work when a service user badly assaulted a member of staff. It had never happened before and there had been no hint of this behaviour from the service user in the preceding months. Following the incident, we held a meeting with the wider staff team to provide an opportunity for them to share their feelings and concerns around the incident. The service was very well managed and enormous consideration was given to keeping staff safe, but there is always learning to take away from these situations. I was conscious throughout the meeting of my instinct to be defensive and bat away any criticism of the organisation. Although everyone remained calm and polite, it felt uncomfortable, and I felt responsible for "allowing" a member of staff to be attacked. I was aware that this provided an opportunity to show the team that I really was open to hearing their concerns and feedback. So, I put my ego to the side and sat and really listened to what was being said. Following the meeting I met with other managers, and we agreed to take several actions forward to improve the safety of staff moving forward. We implemented these actions as soon as possible, not because we were concerned that staff were at risk, but because we wanted to show through our actions that we had listened and did care. It most circumstances you would expect sickness incidents to increase following such an incident, but this was not the case. I believe this was, in part, due to the response of the leadership team in listening to the team's concerns and our willingness to listen and act. This showed staff that they were valued, and we cared.

Reliability is another essential component of trust-building. By setting clear expectations, prioritising accountability, and honouring deadlines, leaders reinforce their reliability and credibility, earning the trust and respect of their colleagues.

Demonstrating Integrity in Actions and Decisions

Integrity is the linchpin of trust, encompassing honesty, consistency, and moral principles. Leaders who uphold high ethical standards and act with integrity inspire trust and confidence among their team members. Aligning actions with values and demonstrating fairness, empathy, and humility cultivate a culture of trust within teams. For example, addressing poor performance can feel uncomfortable, but it upholds work standards and reasserts the boundaries of acceptable behaviour. This increases confidence and trust among team members, who see that the organisations leaders are prepared to do the right thing, even when it feels personally unpleasant.

Integrity is demonstrated not only through words but also through actions. Leaders who lead by example, exhibit consistency, and take ownership of their mistakes inspire trust and respect. By admitting when they are wrong, seeking feedback, and learning from failures, leaders foster a culture of continuous improvement and accountability.

Earning Trust and Respect

Earning trust and respect is a journey that requires patience, humility, and commitment. Leaders must be willing to invest time and effort in building relationships, understanding the needs and concerns of their team members, and leading with empathy and authenticity. By prioritising trust-building efforts, leaders can create a supportive and inclusive environment where individuals feel valued, empowered, and motivated to achieve their full potential.

Conclusion

In conclusion, cultivating trust is a fundamental aspect of effective leadership, essential for fostering collaboration, innovation, and resilience within teams. By embodying honesty, reliability, transparency, and integrity, leaders can earn the trust and respect of their colleagues, laying the foundation for a culture of trust, accountability, and success. Through consistent effort and a genuine commitment to building relationships, leaders can create environments where individuals thrive and organisations flourish.

Practical Actions

- **Be explicit:** Clearly communicate what you are doing and how it aligns with the organisation's values, mission, and goals to avoid assumptions about your motivations.

- **Walk the Walk:** Model the behaviour and integrity you want others to adopt. Follow through on your commitments.
- **Act with integrity:** Do the right thing because it's the right thing, even when you think no one is watching and there's no immediate benefit to you.

CHAPTER 4: NURTURING GROWTH

Nurturing Growth: Empowering Your Team for Personal and Professional Success

In the ever-evolving landscape of leadership, fostering the growth and development of team members is not just a responsibility; it is a profound opportunity to empower individuals to reach their full potential. In this chapter, we delve into the essential principles and actionable strategies for nurturing the growth of your team members, both professionally and personally. By providing opportunities for learning, development, and mentorship, you can cultivate a culture of continuous improvement, innovation, and success.

Understanding the Importance of Growth

Growth is not merely a measure of progress; it is a fundamental aspect of human nature. As leaders, it is our responsibility to create environments where individuals can learn, develop, and flourish. By investing in the growth of our team members, we not only enhance their skills and capabilities but also foster a sense of fulfilment, engagement, and loyalty.

Fostering growth is essential for organisational success in a rapidly changing world. By equipping our team members with the knowledge, skills, and experiences they need to adapt and thrive, we can drive innovation, resilience, and competitiveness within our organisations.

Empowering Individuals to Reach Their Full Potential

Empowering individuals to reach their full potential requires a combination of support, encouragement, and accountability. As leaders, we must create environments where individuals feel valued, challenged, and supported in their endeavours. Individuals need to feel safe to step out of their comfort zone, learn new skills and to get things wrong on the journey.

One key aspect of empowerment is providing opportunities for autonomy and ownership. By delegating responsibilities, empowering decision-making, and fostering a culture of trust and autonomy, we enable individuals to take ownership of their work, pursue their passions, and unleash their creativity and initiative.

Delegating responsibilities is an effective way of increasing employees' confidence. Start by delegating tasks that you are confident the member of staff can complete to a high standard, and gradually introduce more challenging tasks that provide opportunities for greater learning and development. When delegating, focus on the desired outcomes rather than prescribing how the task should be completed. This allows employees the space to find their own path, bringing new perspectives and ideas to the table.

Providing constructive feedback and recognition is essential for empowering individuals to grow and thrive. By offering timely feedback, acknowledging achievements, and celebrating milestones, we reinforce positive behaviours, inspire confidence, and motivate individuals to continue their growth journey. Peer-to-peer feedback can be a useful tool, enabling individuals to gain insights from various perspectives.

The Importance of Investing in Your Team

Enhanced Performance: When team members develop new skills and gain confidence, their performance improves. They become more efficient, effective, and innovative in their roles.

Increased Engagement and Retention: Employees who see that their employer is invested in their growth are more engaged and loyal. This investment reduces turnover and retains top talent.

Building Future Leaders: Developing your team ensures a pipeline of capable leaders within the organisation. This readiness for future leadership roles ensures organisational stability and continuity.

Creating a Positive Work Culture: A culture that promotes growth creates a positive and dynamic work environment. It encourages curiosity, creativity, and collaboration.

Adaptability to Change: In today's rapidly evolving business landscape, having a team that is continually learning and adapting is crucial. It enables the organisation to stay competitive and resilient.

Methods to Encourage Growth

Creating an environment that supports both personal and professional growth requires deliberate strategies and a genuine commitment to your team's development. Here are some effective methods:

Personal Development Plans (PDPs): Work with each team member to create a Personal Development Plan. These plans should outline their career goals, the skills they need to achieve them, and a roadmap for their development. This is often incorporated in an annual appraisal cycle as a method of identifying objectives for the next year.

Continuous Learning Opportunities: Encourage your team to engage in continuous learning through workshops, courses, webinars, and conferences. Providing access to these resources shows your commitment to their growth. By investing in training and development programs tailored to the needs and aspirations of team members, we can enhance their capabilities and performance while demonstrating our commitment to their growth and success.

Informal learning: This plays a crucial role in nurturing growth. Encouraging a culture of curiosity, experimentation, and continuous learning enables individuals to acquire new skills and insights organically through on-the-job experiences, peer-to-peer interactions, and self-directed learning initiatives.

Mentorship: Provides another powerful tool for nurturing growth and development. By pairing team members with experienced mentors who can provide guidance, support, and feedback, we can accelerate their learning and development, facilitate knowledge transfer, and foster meaningful relationships that contribute to their personal and professional growth. Such relationships support the development of both the mentor and mentee.

Cross-Training and Job Rotation: Encourage employees to learn about different roles within the organisation through cross-training or job rotation. This provides opportunity for employees to gain understanding of the roles and challenges facing other aspects of the organisation and to increase their own skills and knowledge. This doesn't have to be undertaken on a grand scale to be effective. In a small organisation this can be achieved by staff working at a time when they wouldn't normally or shadowing a colleague for the day.

Provide Constructive Feedback: Regular feedback is essential for growth. Ensure that feedback is constructive, specific, and actionable. Through this process individuals can gain a greater understanding of their strengths and areas for improvement.

Encourage Work-Life Balance: Personal growth is intertwined with professional growth. Promote work-life balance by encouraging activities that enhance personal well-being and development.

Top Tips for Supporting Growth

1. **Set Clear Expectations:** Clearly communicate what is expected of each team member and how they can achieve those expectations. This clarity helps them set

realistic goals.

Tip: Regularly review job descriptions and performance expectations with your team.

2. **Celebrate Milestones and Achievements:** Recognise and celebrate achievements, both big and small. Celebrating milestones keeps team members motivated and appreciated.

Tip: Create a recognition program where employees are acknowledged for their accomplishments during team meetings or through internal newsletters.

3. **Encourage Autonomy and Ownership:** Empower your team by giving them ownership of their projects and tasks.

Tip: Delegate meaningful tasks and trust your team to make decisions, offering guidance when necessary.

4. **Encourage a Growth Mindset:** Develop a culture where challenges and failures are viewed as opportunities for learning and growth. This resilience is crucial for long-term success.

Tip: Share stories of how setbacks were turned into successes and promote an open dialogue about learning from mistakes.

5. **Support Networking and Collaboration:** Encourage your team to network within and outside the organisation. Collaboration with others can provide new perspectives and ideas.

Tip: Facilitate team-building activities and encourage participation in industry events and professional associations.

Conclusion

Encouraging growth within your team is one of the most impactful investments you can make as a manager. It requires a commitment to continuous learning, a willingness to provide support and resources, and an environment that fosters both personal and professional development. By nurturing growth, you not only empower your team to reach their full potential but also drive your organisation towards greater success. Through our commitment to nurturing growth, we can cultivate environments where individuals thrive, organisations flourish, and the possibilities for innovation and impact are limitless.

Practical Actions

- **Hold regular one-to-one meetings:** Get to know your team members' personal and professional interests and goals to support their growth.

- **Annual Appraisals and Personal Development Plans:** Reflect on the past year, take stock, and develop plans for the next year. Clarity and direction enhance performance.

- **Embed growth in the culture:** Make growth part of every employee's experience, whether through informal learning or formal qualifications. Model a desire to learn and grow as a leader.

CHAPTER 5: CREATING A CULTURE OF FEEDBACK: THE BACKBONE OF A SUCCESSFUL TEAM

Imagine a team where every member feels valued, heard, and empowered to share their insights openly—a place where constructive criticism is welcomed, and praise flows freely. This is not a utopian vision; it is a culture of feedback, the cornerstone of any successful team. Feedback is essential for the growth and improvement of both individuals and organisations. In this chapter, we explore the critical importance of creating a culture of open communication and feedback within teams. By encouraging constructive criticism and actively listening to the perspectives of our team members, we can foster a collaborative environment where everyone feels valued, heard, and empowered to contribute their best.

Understanding the Value of Feedback

Feedback is a powerful catalyst for growth and development, providing individuals with insights into their strengths and areas for continuous improvement. Although the process of giving and receiving feedback can feel uncomfortable to some, it is crucial to incorporate it regularly until it becomes an integral part of the team's daily operations. By creating a culture where feedback is embraced as a means of learning and development, leaders can cultivate environments of trust, transparency, and collaboration.

Feedback is more than just an occasional performance review or a casual comment in a meeting; it is a continuous loop of information that helps individuals and teams grow. A culture of feedback can enhance engagement, drive performance, and build trust, transforming the workplace into a dynamic environment committed to mutual growth and success. Regular feedback provides clear guidance on expectations, helping employees understand how their contributions align with organisational goals. It also allows for timely course corrections, ensuring that small issues are addressed before they become major problems.

Fostering a Culture of Open Communication

Creating a culture of open communication begins with setting the tone from the top. Leaders must lead by example by actively soliciting feedback, demonstrating vulnerability, and responding constructively to input from their team members. Contrary to the belief that admitting mistakes undermines credibility, acknowledging errors gains respect and trust, allowing team members to feel safe making mistakes as well. A leader who cannot acknowledge their weaknesses creates an environment where others feel unable to do the same, hindering growth and transparency. By creating a safe and supportive environment where feedback is welcomed and valued, leaders inspire openness, honesty, and trust among their team members.

Fostering open communication requires establishing channels and mechanisms for feedback to flow freely within the organisation. Whether through regular one-on-one meetings, team meetings, anonymous surveys, or digital platforms, leaders must ensure that team members have opportunities to share their thoughts, ideas, and concerns openly and without fear of retribution. For example, an annual staff survey can track trends over time and provide valuable insights into workplace issues, allowing for informed decision-making and continuous improvement. Additionally, using digital tools like feedback apps can facilitate real-time feedback and make it easier for team members to communicate their thoughts.

Encouraging Constructive Criticism

Constructive criticism is essential for growth and improvement, yet it can be challenging for both givers and receivers. As leaders, it is our responsibility to create conditions where constructive criticism is embraced as a valuable tool for learning and development. One key aspect of encouraging constructive criticism is framing feedback positively and supportively. Instead of focusing solely on areas for improvement, feedback should also highlight strengths and accomplishments, reinforcing a growth mindset and boosting confidence. The "feedback sandwich," where constructive feedback is "sandwiched" between two positive comments, is a classic tool for this purpose.

Additionally, leaders must model resilience and openness in receiving feedback themselves. By demonstrating a willingness to listen, reflect, and act on feedback, leaders set a positive example for their team members and create a culture where feedback is viewed as a two-way street.

Actively Listening to Perspectives

Effective communication is the root of many workplace issues, and active listening is its cornerstone. As leaders, we need to encourage open communication where issues are raised constructively with those involved and not shared behind their back. Active listening involves not only hearing what is being said but also understanding the underlying emotions, motivations, and perspectives behind the message. Leaders can cultivate active listening skills by practicing empathy, maintaining eye contact, and paraphrasing and summarising key points to demonstrate understanding. Creating space for team members to express themselves fully and without interruption fosters deeper connections, builds trust, and encourages collaboration.

Moreover, leaders must be open to feedback from diverse perspectives and experiences. By seeking out input from individuals with different backgrounds, expertise, and viewpoints, leaders can gain valuable insights, challenge assumptions, and make more informed decisions that benefit the entire organisation. This inclusivity in feedback not only enriches the decision-making process but also strengthens the team's cohesiveness and mutual respect. Encouraging team members to share their unique perspectives can lead to innovative solutions and a more dynamic work environment.

Why Feedback Matters

Promotes Growth and Development: Constructive feedback provides employees with a clear understanding of their strengths and areas for improvement. This targeted insight enables them to develop professionally and personally. Employees who receive regular, actionable feedback are better equipped to make informed decisions about their development paths and can take proactive steps to enhance their skills.

Increases Engagement: Employees who receive regular feedback are more engaged. They feel their contributions are noticed and valued, leading to higher job satisfaction and productivity. Engaged employees are more likely to go above and beyond in their roles, contributing to the overall success of the team and organisation.

Builds Trust: When feedback is given and received in a respectful and constructive manner, it fosters trust within the team. This trust is crucial for open communication and collaboration. Teams that trust each other are more likely to share ideas openly, support one another, and work together towards common goals.

Encourages Innovation: A feedback-rich environment encourages creative problem-solving and innovation. Employees feel safe to share unconventional ideas without fear of ridicule. This culture of openness can lead to breakthrough innovations and continuous improvement in processes and products.

Methods to Encourage a Feedback Culture

Creating a culture of feedback is not an overnight process, but with consistent effort and the right strategies, it can be achieved. I have attempted to introduce a range of feedback models in leadership roles. Not all of them have succeeded; some have met with open resistance, forcing me to reflect on their implementation. I have learned that while feedback builds trust in organisations, individuals need to feel safe enough to give feedback in the first place. Some people find giving or hearing constructive feedback difficult, and it can become a superficial and tick-box exercise if left unchecked. Leaders need to be mindful of introducing feedback in a manner that allows everyone to feel safe with the process for it to be meaningful.

When introducing feedback to an organisation initially, I ask colleagues to share what they liked about each other and their behaviour at work before building up to more constructive feedback. This approach helps to create a foundation of trust and positivity, making it easier for individuals to accept and act on more critical feedback later. This can be achieved using the Stop, Start, Continue feedback model which invites individuals to give feedback to others on behaviours they would like them to stop doing, those they would like them to start doing and behaviours they would like them to continue. Depending on your team, their experience and confidence in giving feedback to each other, you may want to consider how to best approach this exercise. A simple, pain free way to introduce the concept is by asking others to begin by saying what they would like their colleagues to continue doing. This can be done face to face or in writing and can be kept between colleagues or shared with the team. I have found having a board where people can write their "continue" feedback to each other for the team to see can be a positive and uplifting experience. Stop and Start feedback is best kept between the individuals involved, at least initially. There are different views on whether this can be done anonymously, with some believing that colleagues will share more meaningful and honest responses if completed this way. However, this does take away from the receiver's ability to consider the feedback in the context of their relationship with the giver and prevents the opportunity for follow up discussion to explore the behaviours and their impact. A quick internet search will generate a lot of information on the model and how it can be used with individuals and teams.

The SBI™ (Situation, Behaviour, Impact) model developed by The Center for Creative Leadership (www.ccl.org) is a valuable feedback model for use in professional as well as personal situations. It's a simple but effective prompt for giving focussed feedback by providing the following prompts:

Situation – putting the feedback in context.

Behaviour – talk about the behaviour you want to address

Impact – highlight the impact of the behaviour.

Here are some other methods to encourage a feedback culture:

Lead by Example: As a manager, your behaviour sets the tone for the team. Regularly seek feedback from your team members and act on it. Show them that feedback is a two-way street.

Example: During team meetings, ask for feedback on your management style or recent decisions. "What could I have done better in managing our last project?"

Regular One-to-Ones: Hold regular one-to-one meetings with your team members. Use these sessions not only to provide feedback but also to solicit it. Ensure these meetings are a safe space for open dialogue.

Example: "I noticed you've been quieter in meetings lately. Is there something on your mind? How can I support you better?"

360-Degree Feedback: Implement a 360-degree feedback system where team members receive feedback from peers, subordinates, and supervisors. This comprehensive approach ensures well-rounded development.

Example: Introduce an anonymous 360-degree feedback survey biannually to capture diverse perspectives on each team member's performance.

Top Tips for Putting Feedback into Practice

Be Specific: Vague feedback is unhelpful. Be clear and specific about what the person did well or what needs improvement.

Tip: Instead of saying, "Good job," say, "Your detailed analysis in the report helped us understand the client's needs better."

Be Timely: Provide feedback as close to the event as possible. Delayed feedback can lose its impact and relevance.

Tip: If you see something that needs addressing, don't wait for the annual review. Address it in your next meeting.

Focus on Behaviour, Not Personality: Feedback should be about actions and outcomes, not personal attributes.

Tip: Avoid statements like, "You're always careless." Instead, say, "The last report had several errors that need attention."

Balance Positive and Negative Feedback: Strive for a balanced approach. Too much criticism can be demoralising, while too much praise can seem insincere.

Tip: Use the "sandwich" method: start with positive feedback, discuss areas for improvement, and end on a positive note.

Encourage Peer Feedback: Foster an environment where team members feel comfortable giving and receiving feedback from each other.

Tip: Create opportunities for peer reviews and group feedback sessions.

Create Actionable Steps: Ensure that feedback leads to action. Work with your team members to develop clear, actionable steps based on the feedback they receive.

Tip: After giving feedback, ask, "What steps can we take to improve this?

Conclusion

Encouraging feedback is essential for creating a collaborative environment where individuals feel empowered to contribute their best and work together toward shared goals. By fostering a culture of open communication, encouraging constructive criticism, and actively listening to the perspectives of our team members, we can build trust, enhance collaboration, and drive Organisational success. Through our commitment to embracing feedback as a catalyst for growth and improvement, we can create environments where everyone has a voice, everyone feels valued, and everyone can thrive

Practical Action:

1. **Implement the Stop, Start, Continue Model:** Use this straightforward feedback approach to guide discussions. Ask team members to identify behaviours they should stop doing, new behaviours they should start, and positive actions they should continue.
2. **Adopt the SBI™ Model for Structured Feedback:** The Situation-Behaviour-Impact™ (SBI) model helps provide clear, specific, and actionable feedback. Focus on describing the context, specific actions, and effects of those actions.
3. **Establish Regular Feedback Mechanisms:** Create formal and informal channels for continuous feedback. Use digital tools, surveys, and regular meetings to facilitate ongoing communication.

CHAPTER 6: LEADING BY EXAMPLE

Ever heard the saying, "actions speak louder than words"? That's the essence of leading by example, a cornerstone principle in the realm of transformational leadership. In this chapter, we explore the profound impact of setting the tone through our actions and embodying the values we wish to instil in our teams.

What is Transformational Leadership

Transactional and Transformational Leadership

When describing the behaviours of a transformational leader Hein, in his 2013 article "How to apply transformational leadership at your company" (available at https://www.cio.com/article/2889761/careers-staffing-how-to-apply-transformational-leadership-at-your-company.html) states "change does not really happen at a company, it happens with people. So, in order to lead change, you have to know how to lead people." He goes on to describe transformational leaders as charismatic, enthusiastic, optimistic, passionate and sometimes visionary. By raising a team's morale and self-confidence, the team can then align itself to an overall vision or common purpose. Transformational leaders encourage the motivation and personal growth of employees, they exemplify moral standards within the organisation and encourage the same of others, such leaders foster a work environment with clear values, priorities, and standards, build a culture where employees are working for the common good and hold emphasis on authenticity, cooperation, and open communication.

Whilst transformational leadership is an exciting, energetic approach to leadership which inspires employees, leading to organisational growth, there is a role for a more transactional leadership approach, and both can be utilised effectively. There are many situations where it is essential during an individual's employment that certain actions happen at specific times to effectively manage and work with the client group. For example, in a hospital it is essential that the right medication is given to the correct person at the right time. The impact of this not taking place could be serious. This aspect of work calls for a transactional leadership approach. However, there may be other areas of work in the same environment where there is the freedom and opportunity to be innovative and creative and where a transformational leadership approach can be adopted.

The Power of Leading by Example

Leading by example is more than just a leadership strategy; it's a philosophy rooted in authenticity, integrity, and accountability. Our behaviours, attitudes, and decisions set the tone for the organisational culture and shape the behaviours of our team members. By embodying the values and principles we espouse, we inspire trust, respect, and loyalty among our followers.

Embodying Kindness

Kindness isn't just a nicety in leadership; it's a powerful force that fuels compassionate leadership. Defined by empathy, compassion, and a generous spirit, kindness has the power to transform workplaces into nurturing environments where everyone thrives. As leaders, we hold the reins to create cultures where kindness isn't just valued; it is celebrated and practiced every day.

Leading with kindness is about more than just lip service; it is about genuine empathy and understanding for others. It's about treating every individual with respect and dignity, creating a sense of inclusivity, and belonging. When we genuinely care about the well-being of our team members, we create an atmosphere where people feel valued, appreciated, and motivated to give their best.

What does this look like in action? For me, it starts with recognising that our employees have lives outside of work. While we expect commitment and reliability during work hours, we also trust our team to manage their time in a way that aligns with their family needs. Whether it's offering flexible hours or accommodating caring responsibilities, prioritising work-life balance is key. In my experience, this flexibility doesn't hinder productivity; it cultivates a motivated, committed team that feels valued and trusted.

It's the small gestures that often make the biggest impact. Allowing employees to leave a couple of hours early to attend a school event or attending a personal appointment without jumping through bureaucratic hoops sends a powerful message of support and understanding. Such acts of kindness not only enrich individual lives but also foster a culture where compassion thrives. As a leader you have an opportunity to influence the organisations culture – your words are important and so are your actions. As a leader simple action such as offering to make colleagues a cup of tea can send a powerful message to others that you value them.

A culture of kindness doesn't just make for a warm and fuzzy workplace; it's a game-changer for morale, engagement, and productivity. When kindness is intrinsic to the way an organisation operates, it creates an environment where people feel valued, respected, and supported. This sense of belonging reduces stress, fosters collaboration, and leads to higher job satisfaction and lower turnover rates.

Leading by example in the workplace is grounded in several key principles that collectively inspire and guide employees towards desired behaviours and attitudes:

Integrity

Leading with integrity in the workplace means consistently adhering to ethical principles and demonstrating honesty, transparency, and fairness in all actions and decisions. Leaders who embody integrity serve as role models, setting a standard for moral behaviour and creating a culture of trust and respect. They communicate openly, honour their commitments, and take responsibility for their actions, including acknowledging mistakes and learning from them. By prioritising integrity, leaders build strong, authentic relationships with their teams, encouraging a work environment where employees feel valued and motivated to uphold the same ethical standards.

Accountability

Modelling accountability as a leader means taking full responsibility for one's actions, decisions, and their outcomes, both positive and negative. It involves setting clear expectations, following through on commitments, and being transparent about progress and setbacks. Accountable leaders admit mistakes without deflecting blame, and they actively seek solutions to rectify issues while learning from the experience. This behaviour establishes a culture of ownership and reliability, where employees feel empowered to take responsibility for their own tasks and contributions.

Commitment

Modelling commitment as a leader means demonstrating unwavering dedication and a strong work ethic in pursuit of the organisation's goals. Committed leaders exhibit persistence, resilience, and a proactive attitude, consistently putting in the necessary effort to overcome challenges and achieve results. They lead by example, showing up prepared, staying focused, and going the extra mile when needed. This dedication inspires and motivates employees to match their level of effort and enthusiasm. However, it is also the role of the leader to model a healthy work life balance, demonstrating hard work as well as boundaries and a commitment to health, wellbeing, family, and friends. In practice this means leaving on time (most of the time), not coming to work when you are too unwell to be there and sharing with colleagues' information about your life outside of work. By doing this, others feel able to leave on time, a culture is established where health and wellbeing is valued, and individuals feel able to show their humanness.

Empathy

Modelling empathy as a leader means actively listening to and genuinely understanding the feelings, perspectives, and concerns of employees. Empathetic leaders create a supportive and inclusive work environment by being approachable and responsive to the needs of their team members. They show compassion and consideration in their interactions, recognising the individuality of each person and valuing their contributions.

Humility

Modelling humility as a leader means recognising and embracing one's limitations and being open to feedback and continuous learning. Humble leaders are approachable and willing to acknowledge their mistakes and shortcomings without defensiveness, demonstrating that they value growth over ego. They give credit to others, celebrate team successes, and prioritise the collective good over personal accolades. By creating an environment where ideas and contributions from all levels are welcomed and appreciated, humble leaders encourage innovation, collaboration, and a culture of mutual respect. This humility not only strengthens relationships within the team but also instils a sense of shared purpose and accountability, driving the organisation towards success.

Positive Attitude

Modelling a positive attitude in the workplace means consistently displaying optimism, enthusiasm, and a solution-oriented mindset, regardless of challenges or setbacks. Leaders with a positive attitude approach problems with a can-do spirit, encouraging their team to view obstacles as opportunities for growth and innovation. They celebrate successes, no matter how small, and maintain morale by focusing on possibilities rather than limitations.

Resilience

Resilience in the workplace is the ability of employees and the organisation to adapt, recover, and thrive in the face of obstacles, setbacks, and changes. It encompasses mental toughness, flexibility, and a proactive attitude towards problem-solving. Resilient employees can maintain productivity and a positive outlook despite difficulties, contributing to a more stable and robust organisational environment. This quality is crucial for navigating the complexities and uncertainties of the modern business landscape, as it enables the workforce to handle stress, innovate, and maintain continuity in operations. Cultivating resilience involves providing support systems, such as training programs, resources for mental health, and fostering a culture that encourages open communication and teamwork.

As leaders, we must embody resilience in our actions and attitudes, demonstrating perseverance, optimism, and determination in the face of obstacles and setbacks. By showing resilience in our own lives and work, we inspire confidence and motivation in others, encouraging them to persevere in the face of challenges and setbacks.

Conclusion

In conclusion, leading by example is a foundational principle of effective leadership, essential for creating environments where individuals thrive, teams excel, and organisations succeed. Through our commitment to leading by example, we can create lasting impact, drive positive change, and leave a legacy of leadership that inspires and empowers others to reach their full potential.

Practical Action:

Lead with Kindness: Start by recognising that employees have lives outside of work. Encourage a culture of flexibility by allowing them to manage their time to fit personal commitments. This fosters trust and shows genuine care for their well-being.

Wellness Action Plans: Consider introducing Wellness Action Plans (WAP) in your organisation for all staff, opening up a dialogue about individual wellbeing and what support employees may find useful. Further information for employers and employees can be found at mind-guide-for-employees-wellness-action-plans_final.pdf

Foster Accountability: Set clear expectations, honour commitments, and admit mistakes when they occur. Create a culture where individuals feel empowered to take ownership of their work, contributing to the success of the organisation.

CHAPTER 7: BALANCING COMPASSION WITH ACCOUNTABILITY

In the intricate dance of leadership, finding the equilibrium between compassion and accountability is both an art and a science. In this chapter, we delve into the delicate balance required to lead with both compassion and accountability, holding our team members to high standards while offering support and understanding when needed. Achieving this balance is crucial for fostering a high-performing and supportive work environment.

The Dance of Compassion and Accountability

Compassion and accountability are often seen as opposing forces in leadership, yet they are intrinsically linked and mutually reinforcing. Compassion without accountability can lead to complacency and underperformance, while accountability without compassion can foster resentment and disengagement. As leaders, it is our responsibility to navigate the tension between these two principles.

Holding our team members to high standards is essential for driving excellence and achieving organisational goals. However, doing so with compassion requires sensitivity, empathy, and a genuine commitment to their growth and development. This approach builds trust and respect, leading to a more engaged and motivated team. Effective leaders understand that holding employees accountable is essential for maintaining standards and achieving organisational goals, but this must be balanced with empathy and understanding.

Setting High Standards with Compassion

Setting high standards with compassion involves clear communication, constructive feedback, and a supportive approach. Excellent communication and kindness are at the core of managing situations that require maintaining a balance between compassion and accountability. Even the most difficult conversations can be managed with kindness, openness, and integrity.

Consider the example of a disciplinary process, a highly stressful experience for an employee. As a leader we can manage the disciplinary process whilst acknowledging the anxiety it may be causing the employee and ensuring they can access appropriate support. Leaders should signpost employees to sources of support, such as an employee assistance program. They should also take care to be explicit about the process that is being followed, one that is likely to be more familiar to them than the employee. By sharing information about the seriousness of the issue and the range of potential outcomes we can help employees prepare and plan. It is possible for individuals to feel respected and valued, even when the process feels uncomfortable, and the outcome is not one they wanted.

Providing Support and Understanding

While holding our team members accountable is essential for driving results, it is equally important to offer support and understanding when needed. Life is unpredictable, and everyone faces challenges and setbacks at some point. The leader's role is to provide a safety net for our team members, offering encouragement, guidance, and assistance when they need it most.

Compassionate leaders are attuned to the needs and

circumstances of their team members, offering flexibility, and understanding when challenges arise. Whether it's providing additional training, adjusting deadlines, or simply lending a listening ear, compassionate leaders create environments where individuals feel valued, supported, and empowered to succeed. This balance between support and accountability not only drives high performance but also fosters loyalty and engagement.

Navigating Tough Conversations with Compassion

Tough conversations are an inevitable part of leadership, whether it's addressing performance issues, delivering unwelcome news, or enforcing consequences for misconduct. Navigating these conversations with compassion requires courage, empathy, and a commitment to preserving dignity and respect.

Approach these conversations with empathy and understanding. Seek to understand the root causes of behaviour or performance issues and offer support and resources to address them. Focus on solutions rather than blame and demonstrate genuine care and concern for the well-being of your team members. This approach fosters trust and collaboration, even in difficult circumstances.

Conclusion

In conclusion, balancing compassion with accountability is a fundamental aspect of effective leadership, essential for creating environments where individuals thrive, teams excel, and organisations succeed. By holding our team members to high standards while offering support and understanding when needed, we create cultures of excellence, integrity, and trust. Through our commitment to compassionate accountability, we can inspire motivation, resilience, and growth in our team members, driving positive change and achieving collective success.

Practical Action:

Establish Clear Expectations and Provide Constructive Feedback: During performance reviews, highlight areas needing improvement and recognise achievements and efforts. Provide specific examples and actionable steps to ensure employees know their contributions are valued while understanding the areas where they need to improve. This fosters a growth-oriented mindset.

Create an Open-Door Policy: Be available and approachable, making it easy for employees to discuss their challenges. Schedule regular one-to-one meetings to check in on their progress and well-being. For instance, if an employee is struggling to meet a deadline due to personal issues, offer flexible working hours or additional resources to help them succeed. This shows you care about their personal circumstances, building loyalty and encouraging a culture of openness and mutual support.

Lead by Example: Demonstrate accountability and compassion in your actions. Admit your own mistakes and take responsibility, setting a powerful example for your team. Show understanding and forgiveness for genuine mistakes to create a safe environment where employees feel encouraged to take risks and innovate without fear of harsh repercussions. This balance cultivates a resilient, high-performing team that feels valued and empowered.

CHAPTER 8: MANAGING CONFLICT WITH GRACE

Conflict is an inevitable aspect of human interaction which cannot and should not be avoided. In this chapter, we explore the art of managing conflict with grace, approaching disagreements and tensions with empathy and diplomacy. By learning effective conflict resolution strategies, leaders can navigate conflicts constructively, fostering harmony and collaboration within their teams.

Understanding the Nature of Conflict

Conflict is an inevitable part of any workplace, arising from diverse personalities, varying perspectives, and the pressure of achieving organisational goals. While conflict is often perceived as negative, it also presents an opportunity for growth, innovation, and deeper understanding. Effective leaders recognise that managing conflict is not about eliminating it but about navigating it constructively. Addressing conflict promptly and thoughtfully prevents minor disagreements from escalating into major disruptions. As leaders, it is our responsibility to recognise and address conflicts proactively, transforming them into opportunities for learning and collaboration. By fostering an environment where open communication is encouraged, leaders can ensure that conflicts are handled in a way that respects all parties involved.

Understanding and Resolving Conflict

To manage conflict effectively, leaders must first understand the root causes. This requires active listening and empathy, allowing leaders to comprehend the underlying issues and emotions driving the conflict. By engaging in honest and transparent conversations, leaders can identify common ground and facilitate collaborative problem-solving. It's crucial to approach these conversations with a mindset geared towards resolution rather than blame, focusing on the facts and the impact of the conflict on team dynamics and productivity. Through this approach, leaders can mediate conflicts in a manner that promotes understanding and cooperation.

In addition to addressing conflicts as they arise, leaders should also take proactive steps to prevent conflicts from occurring in the first place. This involves establishing clear expectations, promoting a culture of respect and inclusivity. It may also include providing training on conflict resolution and communication skills. Leaders can set an example by modelling appropriate behaviour, showing how to handle disagreements respectfully and constructively. By creating a positive and open workplace culture, leaders can minimise the occurrence of conflicts and ensure that when they do arise, they are resolved in a way that strengthens the team and enhances overall performance.

Approaching Conflict with Empathy

Empathy is the foundation of effective conflict resolution, enabling us to understand and validate the perspectives, emotions, and needs of all parties involved. By putting ourselves in the shoes of others and seeking to understand their concerns and motivations, we can create an environment of mutual respect and understanding. Approaching conflict with empathy involves active listening, open-mindedness, and a willingness to suspend judgment. Demonstrating empathy can de-escalate tensions, build trust, and pave the way for constructive dialogue and resolution.

Utilising Diplomacy and Tact

Diplomacy and tact are essential skills for navigating conflicts gracefully and preserving relationships. Instead of resorting to confrontation or aggression, leaders should seek diplomatic solutions that address the underlying issues while maintaining respect and civility. Diplomatic conflict resolution involves finding common ground, exploring win-win solutions, and facilitating open communication and compromise. By remaining neutral, impartial, and respectful towards all parties, leaders can defuse tensions and foster an atmosphere of collaboration and cooperation. Silence can often be more powerful than shouting, allowing space for thoughtful responses rather than reactive outbursts.

Learning Effective Conflict Resolution Strategies

Effective conflict resolution requires a repertoire of strategies and techniques tailored to the specific context and dynamics of each conflict. Some common conflict resolution strategies include:

Active Listening: Listen attentively to the concerns and perspectives of all parties involved, without interrupting or judging. Paraphrase and summarise their points to demonstrate understanding and empathy. Reflecting back what you have heard provides an opportunity for checking understanding and allows the speaker to hear how their perspective sounds. Active listening sounds simple but focusing solely on listening without forming your response at the same time is a learned skill. This skill can be used effectively in one-to-one meetings, providing an opportunity for an individual to talk about things from their perspectives can alone help to diffuse a situation.

Seeking Common Ground: Identify areas of agreement or shared interests that can serve as a basis for resolution. Focus on finding win-win solutions that meet the needs of all involved. Highlighting common goals can unite conflicting parties and pave the way for compromise.

Clarifying Misunderstandings: Address misunderstandings and miscommunications openly and transparently. Encourage clarification and dialogue to ensure that all parties are on the same page. Issues can often arise when individuals make assumptions about the motivations behind another's actions.

Mediation: Facilitate dialogue and negotiation between conflicting parties, acting as a neutral third party to help bridge differences and find mutually acceptable solutions. Effective mediation involves guiding the conversation, keeping it productive, and helping all parties feel heard. I have often been surprised at how quickly issues are resolved once the individuals concerned begin to communicate.

Conflict Coaching: Provide guidance and support to individuals or teams involved in conflict, helping them develop constructive communication and problem-solving skills. This proactive approach can empower team members to handle future conflicts more effectively on their own.

Conclusion

In conclusion, managing conflict with grace is essential for fostering harmony and collaboration within teams. By approaching conflict with empathy and diplomacy and learning effective conflict resolution strategies, leaders can transform conflicts into opportunities for growth, learning, and collaboration. Through our commitment to managing conflict with grace, we can create environments where individuals feel valued, respected, and empowered to work together towards shared goals and aspirations.

Practical Action:

Implement Regular Check-ins: Schedule regular one-to-one and team meetings to discuss ongoing projects and any potential concerns. This proactive approach allows leaders to address minor issues before they escalate into significant conflicts. Encourage an open and honest dialogue where team members feel comfortable sharing their thoughts.

Offer Conflict Resolution Training: Provide training sessions and workshops on conflict resolution and communication skills. Acknowledging that conflict is part of life and equipping your team with the tools to handle conflicts independently helps to create a more harmonious work environment. Include role-playing exercises to practice real-life scenarios and develop effective strategies.

Create a Conflict Resolution Framework: Develop a clear, step-by-step framework for addressing conflicts within your organisation. This framework should include guidelines for reporting conflicts, the process for mediation, and follow-up procedures to ensure resolutions are effective and lasting. Having a structured approach ensures consistency and fairness in handling conflicts.

CHAPTER 9: CELEBRATING SUCCESS

Success, whether big or small, deserves recognition. Celebrating successes, both individual and team achievements, is not just a feel-good exercise but a strategic practice that can significantly boost morale, productivity, and overall team cohesion. As a manager, understanding the importance of celebrating success and how to do it effectively is crucial for building a thriving team. By showing appreciation for their hard work and dedication, we reinforce a positive and supportive work environment where individuals feel valued, motivated, and inspired to excel.

The Power of Celebration

Celebrating success is more than just a feel-good gesture; it is a strategic imperative for driving performance and engagement within teams. When individuals feel acknowledged and appreciated for their contributions, they are more likely to feel motivated, committed, and invested in the success of the organisation.

Moreover, celebration serves as a powerful tool for reinforcing desired behaviours and values within the organisation. By highlighting and honouring achievements that align with the organisation's goals and values, leaders can foster a culture of excellence, innovation, and collaboration.

Recognising Hard Work and Dedication

At the heart of celebration lies recognition – acknowledging the hard work, dedication, and achievements of our team members. Recognition can take many forms, from simple gestures of appreciation to formal awards and ceremonies. In some organisations, food may play a big part in celebrating success – sharing a meal at a celebratory event or providing treats (including healthy options) as a thank you. Regardless of the form it takes, genuine recognition sends a powerful message that individuals' efforts and contributions are valued and appreciated.

Leaders can recognise and celebrate success in many ways, such as publicly acknowledging achievements in team meetings, sending a personalised thank-you note, hosting celebratory events or having a notice board where successes are celebrated. By tailoring recognition efforts to the preferences of team members, leaders can ensure that their efforts resonate and have a meaningful impact.

Reinforcing a Positive Work Environment

Celebrating success plays a crucial role in shaping the organisational culture and climate. When individuals feel recognised and appreciated for their contributions, they are more likely to experience job satisfaction, engagement, and loyalty. Moreover, celebrating success fosters a sense of camaraderie and belonging within teams, strengthening relationships, and enhancing collaboration. This should be inherent in the culture of the organisation, where team members nominate each other for awards, individuals are thanked for doing an excellent job, and positive feedback from external sources is shared with the team.

In addition to boosting morale and motivation, celebrating success also has tangible benefits for organisational performance. Research has shown that organisations that prioritise recognition and celebration experience higher levels of employee engagement, productivity, and retention, as well as improved customer satisfaction and financial performance.

The Positive Impact of Celebrating Success

Boosts Morale and Motivation: Recognition of hard work and achievements boosts team morale. When employees feel valued and appreciated, their motivation to maintain and exceed their performance levels increases.

Enhances Team Cohesion: Celebrating successes together fosters a sense of unity and collaboration. It reinforces the idea that each member's contributions are vital to the team's overall success.

Reinforces Positive Behaviour: Recognising and celebrating achievements reinforces the behaviours and actions that led to success. It encourages employees to continue performing at high levels.

Promotes Job Satisfaction and Retention: Employees who feel acknowledged and appreciated are more satisfied with their jobs. This satisfaction reduces turnover rates and helps retain top talent.

Encourages a Positive Work Environment: Celebrations contribute to a positive and engaging work culture. A workplace that celebrates successes regularly is happier and more productive.

The Pitfalls of Not Celebrating Success

Low Morale and Motivation: When achievements go unnoticed, employees may feel undervalued, leading to decreased motivation and engagement.

Increased Turnover: A lack of recognition can lead to job dissatisfaction, causing valuable employees to seek appreciation elsewhere.

Stifled Innovation: Without recognition, employees may be less inclined to take initiative or propose innovative ideas, fearing their efforts will go unnoticed.

Weakened Team Dynamics: Failure to celebrate team successes can erode the sense of unity and collaboration, leading to a fragmented and less cohesive team.

Negative Work Environment: A culture that neglects to celebrate successes can become negative and demoralising, impacting overall productivity and morale.

Top Tips for Implementing Success Celebrations

1. **Be Specific and Timely:** Recognise achievements as soon as possible. Specific and timely recognition ensures that the praise is meaningful and directly related to the accomplishment. For example, instead of saying "good job," be specific about what the employee did and the impact it had. For instance, "Your detailed report was excellent and helped secure the new client," or "You handled a challenging situation with a service user with sensitivity and patience, which really helped them to calm down and express their needs."

2. **Personalise Recognition:** Tailor your recognition to the individual. Understanding what motivates each team member can make your celebrations more impactful. Not everyone likes public recognition in a team meeting, so consider whether a personal note, email, or one-to-one conversation is more appropriate.

3. **Celebrate Both Big and Small Wins:** While major achievements warrant significant celebrations, don't overlook smaller successes. Regularly acknowledging smaller accomplishments keeps the momentum going.

4. **Encourage Peer Recognition:** Foster a culture where team members also recognise each other's successes. Peer recognition can be incredibly powerful. Some roles will be more visible to managers than others, and this allows for all individuals' input to be recognised and celebrated. This could be done via a weekly or monthly award in a team meeting where individuals

can nominate their colleagues. You could also consider a "Thank You Board" where team members can post notes of appreciation and recognition for their peers.

5. **Make It Inclusive:** Ensure that celebrations are inclusive and recognise the contributions of everyone involved. Team success should be celebrated collectively. For example, if a project is completed successfully, celebrate the entire team's effort with a group lunch or activity.

6. **Tie Recognition to Values:** Align your celebrations with the organisation's values and goals. This reinforces the behaviours that are most important to the organisation.

5. **Be Genuine and Sincere:** Authenticity in recognition is key. Insincere or forced celebrations can have a negative impact and come across as disingenuous. It is crucial that leaders take the time to understand each team member's contribution and express genuine appreciation for their hard work.

6. **Utilise Various Forms of Recognition:** Mix formal and informal recognition. Formal recognition can include awards and certificates, while informal recognition might involve casual praise, and thank-you notes. One idea is to have an annual awards ceremony or "celebratory team meetings" during the year where the focus is on recognising achievements and celebrating success. Depending on the size of your organisation, you could create different award categories that reflect the organisation's goals and values. In addition, a quick email to recognise performance and hard work can have a major impact on an individual. Personally, I have kept all the letters, cards, and thank you emails that have been sent to me over my twenty-five-year career. Even as an established leader, receiving an email saying I did something well gives me a boost.

It may also be appropriate to celebrate success more publicly outside of the organisation by using newsletters or social media to publicly acknowledge achievements. Leaders can also seek opportunities to nominate individuals or teams within their organisations for awards within their industry. This not only recognises the individual or team but also sends a positive message to potential employees, clients, and other stakeholders.

Conclusion

By taking these practical actions, you can create a culture of recognition and celebration that not only acknowledges achievements but also motivates and inspires your team to continue striving for excellence. Embrace the practice of celebrating success, and watch your team flourish and reach new heights

Practical Actions:

Create a Recognition Program: Develop a structured recognition program that includes regular awards for various achievements. Ensure that the criteria for recognition are clear and that the program is communicated effectively to all team members. This program can include monthly awards, annual ceremonies, and spontaneous recognitions for exceptional performance.

Host Regular Celebratory Events: Schedule regular events to celebrate both big and small achievements. These could be monthly team lunches, quarterly outings, or annual parties. Ensure these events are inclusive and cater to the preferences of your team members, making them enjoyable and memorable.

Implement a Peer Nomination System: Encourage team members to nominate their peers for recognition. This system can be facilitated through an online platform or a physical "Thank You Board" where team members can post notes of appreciation. Regularly review these nominations and recognise the contributions in team meetings or through a formal award system.

CHAPTER 10: SUSTAINING COMPASSIONATE LEADERSHIP

Compassionate leadership is not a destination but a journey—a continuous commitment to empathy, understanding, and support. In this chapter, we explore the strategies and practices for sustaining compassionate leadership over the long term. By reflecting on our experiences, seeking feedback, and adapting our leadership style to meet the evolving needs of our teams and organisations, we can create environments where compassion drives, resilience flourishes, and individuals thrive.

Embracing Continuous Learning and Growth

Sustaining compassionate leadership begins with a mindset of continuous learning and growth. As leaders, we must remain open to new ideas, perspectives, and experiences, constantly seeking opportunities for self-reflection and self-improvement.

One way to sustain compassionate leadership is by seeking feedback from our team members, peers, and mentors. By soliciting input on our leadership style, communication effectiveness, and areas for growth, we can gain valuable insights and perspectives that help us refine our approach and become more effective leaders.

Cultivating Resilience and Well-being

Compassionate leadership can be emotionally demanding, requiring us to navigate challenges, setbacks, and conflicts with grace and resilience. To sustain compassionate leadership, it is essential to prioritise our own well-being and resilience, ensuring that we have the energy, motivation, and mental clarity to support our teams effectively.

Practices such as mindfulness, self-care, and stress management can help us recharge and replenish our energy reserves, enabling us to show up as our best selves for our team members. Additionally, seeking support from mentors, peers, or professional coaches can provide valuable guidance and perspective during challenging times. Leadership can feel isolating at times, with even the most experienced feeling the pressure when managing challenging situations. Building relationships with leaders in similar (non-competing) organisations has provided a lifeline for me to safely vent away from the work environment.

Building a Supportive Organisational Culture

Sustaining compassionate leadership requires creating environments where empathy, collaboration, and support are valued and encouraged. Leaders can cultivate a supportive organisational culture by fostering open communication, promoting psychological safety, and modelling vulnerability and authenticity.

By creating spaces where team members feel safe to express themselves, share their concerns, and seek support, leaders can foster a sense of belonging and trust within their teams. Moreover, by championing diversity, equity, and inclusion initiatives, leaders can create environments where all individuals feel valued, respected, and empowered to contribute their unique perspectives and talents.

Adapting to Change and Uncertainty

In today's fast-paced and unpredictable world, sustaining

compassionate leadership requires adaptability and resilience in the face of change and uncertainty. Leaders must be agile and flexible, willing to pivot and adjust their approach in response to evolving circumstances and challenges.

One way to sustain compassionate leadership in times of change is by maintaining a clear sense of purpose and vision. By anchoring ourselves in our core values and principles, we can navigate uncertainty with confidence and clarity, inspiring resilience, and determination in our teams.

Conclusion

Sustaining compassionate leadership is a multifaceted endeavour that requires continuous learning, resilience, and adaptability. By embracing a mindset of growth and self-reflection, prioritising well-being, and resilience, fostering supportive organisational cultures, and adapting to change and uncertainty, leaders can sustain compassionate leadership over the long term. Through our commitment to empathy, understanding, and support, we can create environments where individuals thrive, teams excel, and organisations flourish.

Practical Actions to Sustain Compassionate Leadership

Schedule Regular Reflection Sessions: Dedicate time each week to reflect on your leadership practices. Ask yourself what went well, what challenges you faced, and how you can improve. Keeping a journal can help track your progress and identify patterns over time.

Prioritise Self-Care: Implement daily self-care routines such as exercise, meditation, or hobbies that help you unwind. Make it a habit to check in with yourself and ensure you're not neglecting your own needs while caring for your team. By modelling self-care, you give permission for others in the team to take care of themselves too. A manager who talks the talk, but regularly remains in the office until 10pm at night sends mixed messages about what is valued in the organisation.

Create Feedback Opportunities Establish processes which encourage regular feedback from your team. This can be done through anonymous surveys, one-on-one meetings, or team discussions. Encourage honest and constructive feedback and use it to adapt and improve your leadership style.

www.ingramcontent.com/pod-product-compliance
Lightning Source LLC
Chambersburg PA
CBHW072053230526
45479CB00010B/1001